D0770393

Christmas
The Holiday Journal

A celebration of another season

of love, magic and miracles

in the year

____

Christmas Card List:

Christmas

The Holiday Journal

Christmas Card List:

Christmas
The Holiday Journal

Gifts Given:

Name	Gift

Gifts Received:

Name	Gift

Special foods, recipes, & baked goods:

Christmas

The Holiday Journal

Notes / memorable events of the past year:

Christmas: ____________ (year)

Christmas
The Holiday Journal

The Weather/Temperature was: ____________

Christmas Eve celebrated at / with: ____________

Christmas Day celebrated at / with: ____________

Special cards / gifts given or received: ____________

Parties attended, parties given: ____________

Decorations & trimmings: ____________

Trips, travel, visitors: ____________

Favorite moment, special memories: ____________

Hopes for the New Year: ____________

Photos

A celebration of another season

of love, magic and miracles

in the year

____

Christmas Card List:

Christmas

The Holiday Journal

Christmas
The Holiday Journal

Christmas Card List:

Christmas

The Holiday Journal

Gifts Given:

Name	Gift

Gifts Received:

Name	Gift

Special foods, recipes, & baked goods:

Christmas

The Holiday Journal

Notes / memorable events of the past year:

Christmas

The Holiday Journal

Christmas: ____________ (year)

The Weather/Temperature was: ____________

Christmas Eve celebrated at / with: ____________

Christmas Day celebrated at / with: ____________

Special cards / gifts given or received: ____________

Parties attended, parties given: ____________

Decorations & trimmings: ____________

Trips, travel, visitors: ____________

Favorite moment, special memories: ____________

Hopes for the New Year: ____________

Photos

A celebration of another season

of love, magic and miracles

in the year

____

Christmas Card List:

Christmas

The Holiday Journal

Christmas

The Holiday Journal

Christmas Card List:

Christmas

The Holiday Journal

Gifts Given:

Name	Gift

Gifts Received:

Name	Gift

Special foods, recipes, & baked goods:

Christmas

The Holiday Journal

Notes / memorable events of the past year:

Christmas: ____________ (year)

Christmas
The Holiday Journal

The Weather/Temperature was: ____________

Christmas Eve celebrated at / with: ____________

Christmas Day celebrated at / with: ____________

Special cards / gifts given or received: ____________

Parties attended, parties given: ____________

Decorations & trimmings: ____________

Trips, travel, visitors: ____________

Favorite moment, special memories: ____________

Hopes for the New Year: ____________

Photos

A celebration of another season

of love, magic and miracles

in the year

____

Christmas Card List:

Christmas

The Holiday Journal

Christmas Card List:

Christmas

The Holiday Journal

Gifts Given:

Name	Gift

Gifts Received:

Name	Gift

Christmas

The Holiday Journal

Special foods, recipes, & baked goods:

Notes / memorable events of the past year:

Christmas: ____________ (year)

Christmas
The Holiday Journal

The Weather/Temperature was: ____________

Christmas Eve celebrated at / with: ____________

Christmas Day celebrated at / with: ____________

Special cards / gifts given or received: ____________

Parties attended, parties given: ____________

Decorations & trimmings: ____________

Trips, travel, visitors: ____________

Favorite moment, special memories: ____________

Hopes for the New Year: ____________

Photos

A celebration of another season

of love, magic and miracles

in the year

____

Christmas Card List:

Christmas

The Holiday Journal

Christmas
The Holiday Journal

Christmas Card List:

Christmas
The Holiday Journal

Gifts Given:

Name	Gift

Gifts Received:

Name	Gift

Special foods, recipes, & baked goods:

Christmas
The Holiday Journal

Notes / memorable events of the past year:

Christmas
The Holiday Journal

Christmas: ______________ (year)

Christmas
The Holiday Journal

The Weather/Temperature was: ______________

Christmas Eve celebrated at / with: ______________

Christmas Day celebrated at / with: ______________

Special cards / gifts given or received: ______________

Parties attended, parties given: ______________

Decorations & trimmings: ______________

Trips, travel, visitors: ______________

Favorite moment, special memories: ______________

Hopes for the New Year: ______________

Photos

A celebration of another season

of love, magic and miracles

in the year

____

Christmas Card List:

Christmas
The Holiday Journal

Christmas Card List:

Gifts Given:

Name	Gift

Gifts Received:

Name	Gift

Special foods, recipes, & baked goods:

Christmas
The Holiday Journal

Notes / memorable events of the past year:

Christmas

The Holiday Journal

Christmas: ______________ (year)

Christmas

The Holiday Journal

The Weather/Temperature was: ______________________________

____

Christmas Eve celebrated at / with: ______________________________

____

____

Christmas Day celebrated at / with: ______________________________

____

____

Special cards / gifts given or received: ______________________________

____

____

Parties attended, parties given: ______________________________

____

____

Decorations & trimmings: ______________________________

____

____

Trips, travel, visitors: ______________________________

____

____

Favorite moment, special memories: ______________________________

____

____

Hopes for the New Year: ______________________________

____

____

____

Photos

A celebration of another season

of love, magic and miracles

in the year

____

Christmas Card List:

Christmas

The Holiday Journal

Christmas Card List:

Christmas

The Holiday Journal

Gifts Given:

Name	Gift

Gifts Received:

Name	Gift

Special foods, recipes, & baked goods:

Christmas
The Holiday Journal

Notes / memorable events of the past year:

Christmas: ____________ (year)

Christmas

The Holiday Journal

The Weather/Temperature was: ____________

____

Christmas Eve celebrated at / with: ____________

____

____

Christmas Day celebrated at / with: ____________

____

____

Special cards / gifts given or received: ____________

____

____

Parties attended, parties given: ____________

____

____

Decorations & trimmings: ____________

____

____

Trips, travel, visitors: ____________

____

____

Favorite moment, special memories: ____________

____

____

Hopes for the New Year: ____________

____

____

____

Photos

A celebration of another season

of love, magic and miracles

in the year ____________

Christmas Card List:

Christmas
The Holiday Journal

Christmas Card List:

Christmas
The Holiday Journal

Gifts Given:

Name	Gift

Gifts Received:

Name	Gift

Special foods, recipes, & baked goods:

Christmas
The Holiday Journal

Notes / memorable events of the past year: ______________________

Christmas
The Holiday Journal

Christmas: ____________ (year)

Christmas
The Holiday Journal

The Weather/Temperature was: ____________

Christmas Eve celebrated at / with: ____________

Christmas Day celebrated at / with: ____________

Special cards / gifts given or received: ____________

Parties attended, parties given: ____________

Decorations & trimmings: ____________

Trips, travel, visitors: ____________

Favorite moment, special memories: ____________

Hopes for the New Year: ____________

Photos

A celebration of another season

of love, magic and miracles

in the year

____

Christmas Card List:

Christmas

The Holiday Journal

Christmas Card List:

Gifts Given:

Name	Gift

Gifts Received:

Name	Gift

Christmas

The Holiday Journal

Special foods, recipes, & baked goods:

Notes / memorable events of the past year:

Christmas

The Holiday Journal

Christmas: ______________ (year)

Christmas
The Holiday Journal

The Weather/Temperature was: ______________

Christmas Eve celebrated at / with: ______________

Christmas Day celebrated at / with: ______________

Special cards / gifts given or received: ______________

Parties attended, parties given: ______________

Decorations & trimmings: ______________

Trips, travel, visitors: ______________

Favorite moment, special memories: ______________

Hopes for the New Year: ______________

Photos

A celebration of another season

of love, magic and miracles

in the year

____

Christmas
The Holiday Journal

Christmas Card List:

Christmas Card List:

Christmas

The Holiday Journal

Gifts Given:

Name	Gift

Gifts Received:

Name	Gift

Special foods, recipes, & baked goods:

Christmas

The Holiday Journal

Notes / memorable events of the past year:

Christmas: ______________ (year)

Christmas
The Holiday Journal

The Weather/Temperature was: ______________________________

____

Christmas Eve celebrated at / with: ______________________________

____

____

Christmas Day celebrated at / with: ______________________________

____

____

Special cards / gifts given or received: ______________________________

____

____

Parties attended, parties given: ______________________________

____

____

Decorations & trimmings: ______________________________

____

____

Trips, travel, visitors: ______________________________

____

____

Favorite moment, special memories: ______________________________

____

____

Hopes for the New Year: ______________________________

____

____

____

Photos

A celebration of another season

of love, magic and miracles

in the year

____

Christmas Card List:

Christmas
The Holiday Journal

Christmas Card List:

Christmas
The Holiday Journal

Gifts Given:

Name	Gift

Gifts Received:

Name	Gift

Special foods, recipes, & baked goods:

Christmas

The Holiday Journal

Notes / memorable events of the past year:

Christmas
The Holiday Journal

Christmas: ______________ (year)

Christmas
The Holiday Journal

The Weather/Temperature was: ______________

Christmas Eve celebrated at / with: ______________

Christmas Day celebrated at / with: ______________

Special cards / gifts given or received: ______________

Parties attended, parties given: ______________

Decorations & trimmings: ______________

Trips, travel, visitors: ______________

Favorite moment, special memories: ______________

Hopes for the New Year: ______________

Photos

A celebration of another season

of love, magic and miracles

in the year

____

Christmas Card List:

Christmas Card List:

Christmas
The Holiday Journal

Christmas
The Holiday Journal

Gifts Given:

Name	Gift

Gifts Received:

Name	Gift

Christmas
The Holiday Journal

Special foods, recipes, & baked goods:

Notes / memorable events of the past year:

Christmas: ______________ (year)

Christmas

The Holiday Journal

The Weather/Temperature was: ______________

Christmas Eve celebrated at / with: ______________

Christmas Day celebrated at / with: ______________

Special cards / gifts given or received: ______________

Parties attended, parties given: ______________

Decorations & trimmings: ______________

Trips, travel, visitors: ______________

Favorite moment, special memories: ______________

Hopes for the New Year: ______________

Photos

A celebration of another season

of love, magic and miracles

in the year

____

Christmas Card List:

Christmas

The Holiday Journal

Christmas Card List:

Gifts Given:

Name	Gift

Christmas
The Holiday Journal

Gifts Received:

Name	Gift

Special foods, recipes, & baked goods:

Christmas

The Holiday Journal

Notes / memorable events of the past year:

Christmas

The Holiday Journal

Christmas: ______________ (year)

Christmas — The Holiday Journal

The Weather/Temperature was: ______________________________

____

Christmas Eve celebrated at / with: ______________________________

____

____

Christmas Day celebrated at / with: ______________________________

____

____

Special cards / gifts given or received: ______________________________

____

____

Parties attended, parties given: ______________________________

____

____

Decorations & trimmings: ______________________________

____

____

Trips, travel, visitors: ______________________________

____

____

Favorite moment, special memories: ______________________________

____

____

Hopes for the New Year: ______________________________

____

____

____

Photos

A celebration of another season

of love, magic and miracles

in the year

____

Christmas Card List:

Christmas

The Holiday Journal

Christmas Card List:

Christmas
The Holiday Journal

Gifts Given:

Name	Gift

Gifts Received:

Name	Gift

Special foods, recipes, & baked goods:

Christmas

The Holiday Journal

Notes / memorable events of the past year:

Christmas: ______________ (year)

Christmas
The Holiday Journal

The Weather/Temperature was: ____________________

Christmas Eve celebrated at / with: ____________________

Christmas Day celebrated at / with: ____________________

Special cards / gifts given or received: ____________________

Parties attended, parties given: ____________________

Decorations & trimmings: ____________________

Trips, travel, visitors: ____________________

Favorite moment, special memories: ____________________

Hopes for the New Year: ____________________

Photos

A celebration of another season

of love, magic and miracles

in the year

____

Christmas Card List:

Christmas

The Holiday Journal

Christmas Card List:

Christmas

The Holiday Journal

Christmas
The Holiday Journal

Gifts Given:

Name	Gift

Gifts Received:

Name	Gift

Special foods, recipes, & baked goods:

Christmas
The Holiday Journal

Notes / memorable events of the past year:

Christmas

The Holiday Journal

Christmas: ______________ (year)

Christmas

The Holiday Journal

The Weather/Temperature was: ______________

Christmas Eve celebrated at / with: ______________

Christmas Day celebrated at / with: ______________

Special cards / gifts given or received: ______________

Parties attended, parties given: ______________

Decorations & trimmings: ______________

Trips, travel, visitors: ______________

Favorite moment, special memories: ______________

Hopes for the New Year: ______________

Photos

A celebration of another season

of love, magic and miracles

in the year

____

Christmas Card List:

Christmas Card List:

Christmas
The Holiday Journal

Christmas

The Holiday Journal

Gifts Given:

Name	Gift

Gifts Received:

Name	Gift

Special foods, recipes, & baked goods:

Christmas

The Holiday Journal

Notes / memorable events of the past year:

Christmas
The Holiday Journal

Christmas: ______________ (year)

Christmas

The Holiday Journal

The Weather/Temperature was: ______________________________

____

Christmas Eve celebrated at / with: ______________________________

____

____

Christmas Day celebrated at / with: ______________________________

____

____

Special cards / gifts given or received: ______________________________

____

____

Parties attended, parties given: ______________________________

____

____

Decorations & trimmings: ______________________________

____

____

Trips, travel, visitors: ______________________________

____

____

Favorite moment, special memories: ______________________________

____

____

Hopes for the New Year: ______________________________

____

____

____

Photos

A celebration of another season

of love, magic and miracles

in the year

____

Christmas Card List:

Christmas

The Holiday Journal

Christmas Card List:

Christmas

The Holiday Journal

Gifts Given:

Name	Gift

Gifts Received:

Name	Gift

Christmas
The Holiday Journal

Special foods, recipes, & baked goods:

Notes / memorable events of the past year:

Christmas

The Holiday Journal

Christmas: ____________ (year)

Christmas
The Holiday Journal

The Weather/Temperature was: ____________

____

Christmas Eve celebrated at / with: ____________

____

____

Christmas Day celebrated at / with: ____________

____

____

Special cards / gifts given or received: ____________

____

____

Parties attended, parties given: ____________

____

____

Decorations & trimmings: ____________

____

____

Trips, travel, visitors: ____________

____

____

Favorite moment, special memories: ____________

____

____

Hopes for the New Year: ____________

____

____

____

Photos

A celebration of another season

of love, magic and miracles

in the year

____

Christmas Card List:

Christmas Card List:

Christmas

The Holiday Journal

Christmas

The Holiday Journal

Gifts Given:

Name	Gift

Gifts Received:

Name	Gift

Special foods, recipes, & baked goods:

Notes / memorable events of the past year:

Christmas: ____________ (year)

Christmas — The Holiday Journal

The Weather/Temperature was: ____________

Christmas Eve celebrated at / with: ____________

Christmas Day celebrated at / with: ____________

Special cards / gifts given or received: ____________

Parties attended, parties given: ____________

Decorations & trimmings: ____________

Trips, travel, visitors: ____________

Favorite moment, special memories: ____________

Hopes for the New Year: ____________

Photos

A celebration of another season

of love, magic and miracles

in the year

____

Christmas Card List:

Christmas Card List:

Christmas
The Holiday Journal

Gifts Given:

Name	Gift

Gifts Received:

Name	Gift

Special foods, recipes, & baked goods:

Notes / memorable events of the past year:

Christmas

The Holiday Journal

Christmas: ____________ (year)

Christmas
The Holiday Journal

The Weather/Temperature was: ______________________________

____

Christmas Eve celebrated at / with: ______________________________

____

____

Christmas Day celebrated at / with: ______________________________

____

____

Special cards / gifts given or received: ______________________________

____

____

Parties attended, parties given: ______________________________

____

____

Decorations & trimmings: ______________________________

____

____

Trips, travel, visitors: ______________________________

____

____

Favorite moment, special memories: ______________________________

____

____

Hopes for the New Year: ______________________________

____

____

____

Photos

A celebration of another season

of love, magic and miracles

in the year

____

Christmas Card List:

Christmas

The Holiday Journal

Christmas Card List:

Christmas

The Holiday Journal

Christmas

The Holiday Journal

Gifts Given:

Name	Gift

Gifts Received:

Name	Gift

Special foods, recipes, & baked goods:

Christmas

The Holiday Journal

Notes / memorable events of the past year:

Christmas

The Holiday Journal

Christmas: ____________ (year)

Christmas
The Holiday Journal

The Weather/Temperature was: ____________

Christmas Eve celebrated at / with: ____________

Christmas Day celebrated at / with: ____________

Special cards / gifts given or received: ____________

Parties attended, parties given: ____________

Decorations & trimmings: ____________

Trips, travel, visitors: ____________

Favorite moment, special memories: ____________

Hopes for the New Year: ____________

Photos

A celebration of another season

of love, magic and miracles

in the year

____

Christmas Card List:

Christmas

The Holiday Journal

Christmas Card List:

Christmas
The Holiday Journal

Christmas

The Holiday Journal

Gifts Given:

Name	Gift

Gifts Received:

Name	Gift

Special foods, recipes, & baked goods:

Christmas

The Holiday Journal

Notes / memorable events of the past year:

Christmas: ______________ (year)

Christmas
The Holiday Journal

The Weather/Temperature was: ______________

Christmas Eve celebrated at / with: ______________

Christmas Day celebrated at / with: ______________

Special cards / gifts given or received: ______________

Parties attended, parties given: ______________

Decorations & trimmings: ______________

Trips, travel, visitors: ______________

Favorite moment, special memories: ______________

Hopes for the New Year: ______________

Photos

A celebration of another season

of love, magic and miracles

in the year

____

Christmas Card List:

Christmas

The Holiday Journal

Christmas Card List:

Gifts Given:

Christmas

The Holiday Journal

Name	Gift

Gifts Received:

Name	Gift

Special foods, recipes, & baked goods:

Christmas
The Holiday Journal

Notes / memorable events of the past year:

Christmas

The Holiday Journal

Christmas: ______________ (year)

Christmas
The Holiday Journal

The Weather/Temperature was: ____________________

Christmas Eve celebrated at / with: ____________________

Christmas Day celebrated at / with: ____________________

Special cards / gifts given or received: ____________________

Parties attended, parties given: ____________________

Decorations & trimmings: ____________________

Trips, travel, visitors: ____________________

Favorite moment, special memories: ____________________

Hopes for the New Year: ____________________

Photos

A celebration of another season

of love, magic and miracles

in the year

____

Christmas Card List:

Christmas

The Holiday Journal

Christmas

The Holiday Journal

Christmas Card List:

Christmas
The Holiday Journal

Gifts Given:

Name	Gift

Gifts Received:

Name	Gift

Christmas
The Holiday Journal

Special foods, recipes, & baked goods:

Notes / memorable events of the past year:

Christmas

The Holiday Journal

Christmas: ______________ (year)

Christmas
The Holiday Journal

The Weather/Temperature was: ______________

Christmas Eve celebrated at / with: ______________

Christmas Day celebrated at / with: ______________

Special cards / gifts given or received: ______________

Parties attended, parties given: ______________

Decorations & trimmings: ______________

Trips, travel, visitors: ______________

Favorite moment, special memories: ______________

Hopes for the New Year: ______________

Photos

A celebration of another season

of love, magic and miracles

in the year

____

Christmas Card List:

Christmas
The Holiday Journal

Christmas Card List:

Christmas

The Holiday Journal

Gifts Given:

Name	Gift

Gifts Received:

Name	Gift

Christmas

The Holiday Journal

Special foods, recipes, & baked goods:

Notes / memorable events of the past year:

Christmas

The Holiday Journal

Christmas: ______________ (year)

Christmas
The Holiday Journal

The Weather/Temperature was: ______________________________

____

Christmas Eve celebrated at / with: ______________________________

____

____

Christmas Day celebrated at / with: ______________________________

____

____

Special cards / gifts given or received: ______________________________

____

____

Parties attended, parties given: ______________________________

____

____

Decorations & trimmings: ______________________________

____

____

Trips, travel, visitors: ______________________________

____

____

Favorite moment, special memories: ______________________________

____

____

Hopes for the New Year: ______________________________

____

____

____

Photos

The "Write It Down!"® Series
Journals Unlimited, Inc.

With over 50+ titles, there is something for everyone.

- Vacation
- Camping
- Boating
- Golfing
- Birthday
- Christmas
- Sledding
- Me (personal)
- Fishing
- Hunting
- Guest
- Gardening
- Teachers
- Up North (Cabin)
- Daily Devotions
- Blank
- Email
- Contacts
- Girls Only
- Mom
- Dream
- R & R (Cottage)
- Memories
- Dining Out
- Wine
- Readers
- Hiking
- Skiing
- Recipe
- Birdwatchers
- Films & Movies
- Me Myself & I
- Inspirations (Gratitude)
- Motorcycle
- My Story (Wellness)
- Destinations (Lighthouse)
- Sketch
- Treasures
- Horses
- Lighten Up
- Baseball
- Basketball
- Football
- Hockey
- Soccer
- Campus Life
- Paddling (Canoe-Kayak)
- Wild Things
- Cruise
- Homeowners
- Dinner Parties

Still can't find what you're looking for?
We offer **CUSTOM DESIGNED JOURNALS.**

- **Employee Incentives**
- **Company Premiums/Promotions**
- **In-store Product**
- **Gifts to Customers or Employees**
- **Fund-raisers**
- **Charitable Donations**
- **Special Events**
- **Event Sponsorships**

For more information regarding this service please visit:

www.customjournals.net